S0-ABA-359

Christine Carter

Supermom Series

Toddler Discipline: Essential Guide

for Parents

All rights Reserved.
No part of this publication or the information in it may be quoted from or reproduced in any form by means such as printing, scanning, photocopying or otherwise without prior written permission of the copyright holder.

Disclaimer and Terms of Use:
Effort has been made to ensure that the information in this book is accurate and complete, however, the author and the publisher do not warrant the accuracy of the information, text and graphics contained within the book due to the rapidly changing nature of science, research, known and unknown facts and internet. The Author and the publisher do not hold any responsibility for errors, omissions or contrary interpretation of the subject matter herein. This book is presented solely for motivational and informational purposes only.

Table of Contents

Introduction

Hello Supermoms! Welcome to your Ultimate Guide to Toddler Discipline.

Toddlerhood is an exciting time. Your baby is gaining an important sense of self, exploring her identity, learning to make decisions, discovering likes and dislikes, and hitting important milestones in language, cognitive, and social development.

As your baby moves into toddlerhood, it may at times seem that your little one has gone from adorable, cooing infant to overly emotional, unpredictable tyrant overnight. With terms like 'the terrible twos' coming into play, it's no wonder that many new parents feel overwhelmed during this stage of their baby's development.

However, there's no need to fear! Although the toddler years can sometimes be frustrating for both toddlers and moms, it's also an exciting time full of growth and fun.

Your relationship with your baby will deepen in new and enjoyable ways as you experience the ups and downs of emerging selfhood together.

As your toddler begins to exert independence in his interactions with you and others, helping him to develop discipline will become vital to his success individually and socially. The toddler years are an important time for you to lay groundwork for skills in emotional regulation and social interaction, as well as instill behaviors that will set your child up for success as he prepares to enter the school years.

Some of the questions that will be answered in this book include:

- How does brain development relate to toddler discipline?
- What kinds of limits does a toddler need or not need?
- How can you develop healthy communication patterns with your little one?
- What are the best ways to help toddlers learn to deal with conflict?
- What discipline strategies are most effective in helping toddlers through this crucial stage of development?
- How can you as a Supermom stay calm in the face of toddler frustration?

As you move through the book and the answers to these questions, you'll find numerous tips and tricks to help you apply what you learn in real-world situations.

You'll also discover that we've included insights from a variety of perspectives, because when it comes to toddler discipline, there is no such thing as 'one size fits all.' Each and every toddler has unique needs and temperament, so it's important to find the strategies that work for *your* child. The Supermom Series is here to help you do just that.

Let's get started!

Chapter 1:

Brain Development and Why It Matters

Your child is growing quickly between 1 and 4 years of age, but not just in height and weight. When it comes to toddler discipline, it's crucial to gain a basic understanding of how your little one's brain and character are blossoming. Throughout toddlerhood, your baby will progress through important steps in both of these areas of development.

Developmental factors will play a direct role in what kinds of behaviors you might expect to see from your child. They will also impact how you respond to unproductive behaviors over time and how you help your toddler to learn the skills and self-regulation needed to grow into healthy, happy, functioning individuals.

Child development is an exciting and growing field of study. An in-depth look at all of the fascinating aspects of toddler brain development is outside the scope of this book, but a basic understanding of what's going on in your child's mind at different ages will help you to make the best decisions about how to interact with and encourage your little one's growing sense of independence.

Knowing what to expect and why certain behaviors happen will also help minimize your own frustration when baby 'misbehaves.'

In the following section, we will touch on some of the most important developmental achievements as they relate to toddler discipline from ages 1-4. However, don't worry if your toddler hasn't checked off every item in every category; each child develops at his or her own pace and may reach certain milestones faster or slower than the 'average' toddler. If you are concerned, or if your toddler seems particularly behind her peers, always consult a pediatrician to make sure that everything is on track.

12-18 Months: During this time, your toddler will begin to use the word 'no,' as well as make requests and follow simple, single-step instructions. She has little, if any, in the way of impulse control or emotional self-regulation. With her newfound mobility, she will begin to venture out and explore her environment on her own, although she will usually still need the reassurance of mom's presence. As she begins to assert her independence by expressing her wants and engaging in more independent activity, gentle discipline strategies will help her to stay safe and healthy.

The table below summarizes key milestones in brain and social/emotional development:

	Brain Development	Social/Emotional Development
by 12 – 18 months	- Expresses 'no' - Expresses desire (i.e. through pointing) - Recognizes everyday concrete objects such as bottles, blankets, and books - Can follow single-step verbal commands such as 'sit down' or 'come here.'	- May begin to have temper tantrums - May begin to show a fear of strangers - Shows affection for others - May cling to mom, especially around strangers or in unfamiliar situations - Uses pointing to share interesting finds with others - Begins to explore by venturing out alone, usually as long as a caregiver/ parent is present

18 Months – 2 Years: Your little one is well into toddlerhood. By now, he is starting to speak in short sentences, show an increased interest in other children, engage in simple imaginative play, and follow more complex instructions. He can also recognize the names of objects or pictures of objects and point to them when prompted. By this age, he is able to experience the full range of emotions. Thanks to his burgeoning independence, more fully developed emotions, and lack of impulse control or emotional regulation, tantrums and refusals will begin to occur. Discipline strategies will continue to be focused on keeping your toddler safe and healthy, while helping them to develop self-control. Check out the table below for a more in-depth look.

	Brain Development	Social/Emotional Development
by 2 years	- Points to things or pictures when they are named - Able to form short sentences (2-4 words) - Begins to be able to sort basic shapes and colors - Begins to play rudimentary make-believe games - Can follow instructions with two steps	- Mimics the words and behavior of others - Gets excited when around other children - Increases in independence - Shows defiant behavior - For the most part, plays next to other children rather than with them, but is beginning to include other children in simple games such as chase

2-3 Years: By now, your toddler is exhibiting increasingly complex cognitive abilities, including following more complicated instructions and completing simple puzzles. He is also able to hold short conversations with full sentences and demonstrates enjoyment of and empathy for others. He's grown more socially independent, separating from parents with greater ease. The terrible twos have arrived full force, and you can expect more resistance when your toddler is tired or doesn't get his or her way. As with all stages of toddlerhood, discipline will continue to focus on health and safety, but now you can begin to introduce more concrete life skills such as sharing, turn taking, and better emotional regulation.

	Brain Development	Social/Emotional Development
by 3 years	- Can follow instructions with 3 steps - Can hold a short conversation using 2 to 3 sentences - Can play with more complicated toys that include moving parts - Engages in imaginative play with people and toys - Can complete very simple puzzles	- Copies the behavior of others - Shows affection for others - Engages in turn-taking during games and other activities - Shows concern for friends or family in distress - Understands possession ('mine' vs 'his' or 'hers') - Shows a wide range of emotions - Able to explore comfortably without a caregiver's presence at least some of the time - May be upset or uncomfortable with changes in routine

3-4 Years: The skills that began to appear between 12 and 36 months will continue to develop, leading your toddler to be able to engage in more complex cognitive activities, such as memorizing nursery rhymes and beginning to conceptualize things like time and contrast. She may also show an awe-inspiring degree of creativity as she engages in imaginative play with herself, her toys, and others. By now, she's probably learned a degree of self-control when it comes to emotional regulation and is having fewer/shorter tantrums. She's made strides in impulse control, although it's still very much a work in progress. She has also learned to meet basic behavioural expectations, such as not throwing food, not hitting, and cleaning up toys. During this stage of development, discipline will become more focused on helping your toddler to learn the foundations of critical life skills such as cooperation and conflict resolution.

Age	Brain Development	Social/Emotional Development
by 4 years	- Abel to recite simple songs and poems from memory - Abel to tell stories and make predictions in a story - Understands the concept of counting and may be able to count - Begins to understand the concept of time - Understands the concept of 'same' and 'different'	- Becomes increasingly creative with imaginative play - Enjoys playing with other children more than playing alone - Is able to cooperate with other children - Not always able to tell what's real and what's make-believe - Talks about likes and interests

As you can see, the toddler years are a crucial time for brain and social development. As your child moves through each stage of toddlerhood, there some important supportive and risk factors to keep in mind to ensure your little one's optimal brain and social development.

Supportive factors are environmental, situational, and interpersonal influences which contribute to and/or support healthy development. *Risk factors*, on the other hand, may have an unhealthy, detrimental, or damaging effect on your child's brain and social/emotional development.

The table below lists some of the supportive and risk factors to look out for. Supportive factors should be encouraged within the home and risk factors minimized or eliminated.

Supportive Factors	Risk Factors
- Responsive caregiver interactions (caregiver interprets and responds to toddler's emotions/needs in an accurate and timely manner) - Loving interactions - Hugs - Adequate nutrition - Healthy sleep - Time for safe exploration in a caregiver's presence - Structure and routine	- Lack of loving interaction from mother or primary caregiver - Invasive or unresponsive parenting - Too much 'screen time' - Poor nutrition - Poor sleep - Stress in the home - Abuse of the toddler - Abuse in the toddler's presence

Now that we've gone over some of the exciting developmental steps you can expect to see throughout toddlerhood, it's time to move on to the next aspect of our discussion on toddler discipline: Limits!

*developmental tables adapted from information found at www.cdc.gov/ncbddd/actearly/milestones/index.html

Chapter 2:

Toddlers Need Limits! Or Do They?

Your baby's mobility has opened a whole new world of exploration and experience. She will begin to take initiative, make requests, and experiment within her environment. As your toddler begins to make her needs and wants known in increasingly insistent ways, an important question arises: Just how much should you give your baby what she wants?

When Jessa, age 30 months, repeatedly refused to pick up her toys before snack time, her mother Karen was at a loss. The tantrums that erupted anytime Karen insisted that Jessa help clean up the mess before having a snack were exhausting. Karen finally started just handing out the snack first and then cleaning things up herself, rather than having to deal with her upset toddler. She knew Jessa was capable of picking up the toys, and she wanted to help her learn. But it was easier and less stressful to pick up the toys herself.

Karen's is a familiar conundrum for most of us. The truth is, setting limits can be difficult—even exhausting—for parents.

Why Set Limits

The time you spend helping your toddler to learn age-appropriate limits and boundaries is time well spent. Not only will healthy limits make your life easier in the long run, they are also a vital part of your little one's development. There are many benefits to setting healthy limits for your toddler, including:

Limits provide structure. Limits provide added structure and order to a toddler's world by helping her to know what to expect in different situations. Much as routine helps toddlers by lending predictability to their world, limits give toddlers the comfort of knowing what is expected of them.

Limits promote success. When there are no limits, toddlers encounter failure far more often than is necessary for growth. Allowed to run rampant, unregulated impulses, emotions and behaviors will lead to stress and conflict as the toddler attempts to interact with others and with their environment. Limits give toddlers more opportunities to succeed by teaching them appropriate, successful behaviors for various situations. For example, teaching a child not to hit when they are angry will protect them from being hit back and keep conflict at a more manageable level, protecting their playtime and their relationships.

Limits boost confidence. As your toddler learns to achieve her goals within the healthy limits you've set for her, she will experience an increased sense of confidence in her own choices and abilities. Thanks to limits, she will begin to see cause and effect between behaviors that don't work and behaviors that do. Her growing understanding will help her to make sense of the world and her ability to make choices within it.

Limits provide teaching opportunities. It can be hard to set limits after a long day. In the moment, it is often faster, easier, and less stressful to give in to a toddlers' demands or let them get away with things that you'd rather not. However, setting limits is about more than just reinforcing good behavior. Each time you set a limit with your toddler, you have the opportunity for a teaching moment. For example, helping children learn to try the food on their plates is also an opportunity to teach them about the importance of keeping an open mind, appreciation for those who do kind things for us, and developing our likes and dislikes.

Limits prepare toddlers for the 'real world.' As toddlers grow into children, they will be faced with all of the expectations and consequences that come with social interaction in a community. Learning to regulate their emotions, follow instructions, and work with others will help them to succeed as they venture out into the school and community.

Limits keep toddlers safe. In some cases limits are necessary to ensure your little one's safety. For example, teaching toddlers not to climb up bookshelves or dig in the trash will help them to avoid accident or illness.

Limits keep toddlers healthy. In a modern world where far too many of us face the diseases of civilization, limits can help keep toddlers healthy. It can be tempting to give in to a 3-year-old's demands for ice-cream and cookies, but by setting limits on these types of unhealthy foods, you can help your toddler learn to self-regulate his food choices.

Limits help toddlers learn to socialize. Once toddlers start interacting with other children, they will need to engage in social behaviors such as sharing, turn-taking, resolving conflicts, and listening. Setting limits will help your toddler learn to socialize in ways that lead to healthy, enjoyable relationships and successful social interactions.

Why Toddlers Push Limits

You've chosen the most developmentally appropriate, growth promoting limits possible. You've carefully considered which ones are really necessary and are being careful not to over-restrict. You've set up and consistently enforced the limits as lovingly as possible...so why does your toddler keep pushing?

The short answer is, it's normal! Even the most skilled gurus of toddler discipline cannot eliminate push-back, nor should they—testing boundaries is an important part of your toddler's development. Sometimes, pushing back is indicative of a problem, but usually, it's simply normal toddler behavior.

Toddlers lack both impulse control and much ability to regulate their own emotions. Combine these facts with the intense ups and downs of emotion that most children experience, and it becomes a little easier to understand why they sometimes (or often) have difficulty resisting the urge to throw toys, hit a sibling out of frustration, have tantrums, or simply reach out and poke that one thing you've told them repeatedly not to touch.

It can't be stressed enough how important it is not to take these behaviors personally. Pushing back on boundaries is not only normal, your toddler truly can't help it much of the time. Self-control is an ever-evolving process, and will only come with time, love, and learning. Taking pushback personally adds unnecessary stress to a parent's life and limits opportunities for effective teaching.

There are a number of reasons why your toddler may push limits. Being aware of them can help us to maintain perspective in the more frustrating moments and deal with them more effectively. Let's take a look at some common reasons behind pushing back.

Experimentation. In the beginning, a toddler may not be convinced that she's *really* not allowed to climb up on the piano. Her repeated attempts to do what you've told her not to could be just plain old fashioned experimentation. '*Will mommy stop me this time? What about this time? What about if I try it while she's cooking? What about now?*' In these situations, staying calm, firm, and most of all consistent will help your toddler realize that the rule is not going to change.

In need of help. None of us like feeling tired, hungry, stressed, or overwhelmed. As adults, we've developed a variety of coping mechanisms to deal with these conditions, but your little one is still learning how to face the difficulties of life as a human. Sometimes, pushing on limits is the result of your toddler needing help and not knowing how to ask for it.

Just as you would take a moment to check your baby's diaper or hunger and thirst levels in response to crying, it's a good idea to take a moment and check in with your toddler's physical and emotional condition if they're pushing limits— especially if they also seem grumpy and out of sorts. In these situations, pushback can often be reduced or even eliminated simply by taking care of an unmet need.

Reassurance. Sometimes, toddlers need to be reassured that parents are reliable and that the world as they know it can be trusted to behave as expected. They push limits because they want to know that we will respond in predictable ways.

Teasing and play. Toddlers love to play, giggle, and have fun. Sometimes, they push limits simply to tease and laugh, or because they think it's a game. This behavior can occur on its own, but it can also be the result of mixed signals from a caregiver. Although toddlers can sometimes misbehave in the most adorable ways, giggling in response to cuteness when toddlers push limits can give the impression that misbehavior is a game.

For example, when 2-year-old Marie hit a friend during play, her mother Lisa, who was sitting with the children, said, *'No Marie. We don't hit.'* Marie teasingly slapped Lisa's knee in response. The mischievous grin and good humor on Marie's face caused Lisa to smile in amusement. Enjoying the attention, Marie slapped her mother's knee again. Not wanting to take away from her daughter's good mood, Lisa continued to say *'No, we don't hit'* even as her facial expressions and body language said *I like what you're doing.*

If you find yourself stuck in such a cycle while trying to set a limit, you can get things back on track by using clear body language that matches your intent. In this case, Lisa took Marie's hands in her own and made eye contact. Then, with a neutral expression on her face, she shook her head no and said, *'That's enough. We don't hit, okay?'* and waited for Marie to nod before letting go.

Attention. When toddlers feel ignored or unimportant, they often act out for attention. One way of doing this is to push limits. Sometimes, simply scooping them up for a moment of cuddle time or a story is all they need to get back to normal.

Love. Hand in hand with the need for attention is the need to feel loved. If your toddler is pushing back, he may simply need the reassurance of a hug and the knowledge that you love him. Don't be afraid to tell him often how much you care about him.

Tips for Setting Limits

So just how does one go about setting effective limits? The following tips will help you to set limits in ways that encourage growth and avoid authoritarianism.

Tip 1: Be consistent. When you set a boundary, be prepared to enforce that boundary on a regular basis. Boundaries that are firmly enforced one day and irrelevant the next hold little meaning for a toddler. By being consistent, your toddler will learn to respect the limit more quickly. He will also benefit from the structure and predictability that consistently enforced boundaries provide.

Tip 2: Know when to say yes. I know, we just said that it's important to be consistent. However, there will occasionally be times when it's appropriate or necessary to make an exception to a boundary or limit. For example, if your toddler is usually allowed one popsicle/day, a sore throat may make room for an extra. Knowing when to say yes shows your toddler that limits are important for our lives because they reasonable, not because they are arbitrary.

Tip 3: Use limits wisely. Toddlers are naturally scientists, exploring and experimenting with the world around them nearly every waking moment. They are constantly learning, discovering, and formulating. The ability to engage in these activities as they make independent choices is vital to their development and happiness. While some limits contribute to a toddler's development, too many restrictions can be just as detrimental as none. Limits should promote health, safety, social development, and emotional regulation without overly restricting the toddler's ability to play, explore, and make choices.

Tip 4: Be firm but gentle. Being too passive communicates to your toddler that you're not really serious about the limit being set, or that you don't care. Explain the limit in simple, age-appropriate language, in a firm but gentle tone while making eye contact. Don't become aggressive or be overly passive or distracted while setting limits.

Tip 5: Listen. Limits will sometimes cause frustration for your child. Listen to their frustrations, validate them, be willing to explain the purpose of the limit, and be prepared to help them navigate limits with distractions and alternatives. By listening and responding with care and consideration, you will teach your toddler that you are their partner in success.

Approaching limits with positivity and love will help you get the most out of them. When limits are set effectively, they do far more than just enforce desirable behavior. They also help your toddler to develop important self-regulation skills, provide a physically and emotionally safe structure in which to explore, and develop both confidence and self-awareness. Maintaining limits can be challenging, but investing the time and energy to do so will save you frustration down the line and set your toddler up for success in the coming school years.

Chapter 3:

Communication is Vital

Communication is key in any relationship, and the one you have with your baby is no different. The period from ages 1 through 4 is vital to your toddler's emerging language and social skills. Parent-child communication during this stage of development is all about effective interaction, modelling communicative behaviors, and fostering confidence, safety, and self-development.

The first thing to remember about communicating with your toddler is that it is a *dynamic, two-way interaction*. One reaches out, the other responds. As you and your toddler learn to interact in increasingly responsive and effective ways, he will develop an increased sense of safety, confidence, empathy, and self-determination.

Let's consider some of the key components of effective communication.

Effective Communication: Talking

The way that a parent speaks communicates much more than simply words. When you engage verbally with your toddler, you are modelling how a conversation works, including important skills such as listening, empathy, and turn-taking. As toddlers observe you talking to themselves and others, what they learn about human interaction contributes to their understanding of what it means to communicate effectively and exist in a social context.

But setting a good example isn't the only thing to keep in mind. The way that parents speak to their toddlers also impacts how effective the communication is (does the toddler understand in a way that is actionable?) and the toddler's developing emotional and social understanding.

Talking to your toddler in ways that are too aggressive or too passive can have negative consequences on their emotional and social development as well as detract from the potential benefits of teaching moments and healthy discipline. Rather, parents should speak firmly but kindly as they seek to communicate with their toddlers.

With these key points in mind, let's consider some important tips for talking in ways that your toddler can understand:

Tip 1: Use eye contact. When talking with your toddler, don't expect them to listen or understand if you're really just talking *at* them. Set aside any distractions, make eye contact, and let yourself connect fully with your little one. Eye contact will help your toddler to pay attention to what you're saying and stay engaged in the conversation. It will also help bolster their sense of personhood by making it clear that you are interested in them.

Tip 2: Speak to them by name. Using your toddler's name while talking with them is another way to keep them focused on the conversation and give them a sense of importance as a co-communicator. It's especially good to use names when validating or when you're trying to let them know that you approve or disapprove. For example, *'Wow Jonny, that sounds so frustrating,'* or *'I love how you shared with your sister, Alex,'* or *'We don't throw food David—please stop.'*

Tip 3: Don't yell. Once you start yelling, chances are that your toddler's behavior will become worse, either right then and there or manifested the next day or week. Yelling sets a poor example for your toddler and is likely to cause them stress that could become damaging. You may also frighten them, further adding to their anxiety and fueling further misbehavior as they try to cope. Instead, speak in a calm bit firm voice. If needed, take a moment to breathe and calm down before speaking.

Tip 4: Be assertive, but not aggressive. As was discussed in the limits chapter, sometimes kids misinterpret our responses and may not realize that we are serious about a limit, or may think that we are engaging in play. Be clear about the purpose of your communications by using an assertive tone and body language when appropriate. However, do not mistake assertiveness for aggression. Assertiveness effectively communicates ideas and expectations, aggressiveness communicates danger, fear, and dislike.

Tip 5: Smile. Babies and toddlers are particularly responsive to facial expressions. As you no doubt discovered during the first year, sometimes a well-directed smile is all that it takes to brighten up a discontented baby. The same holds true for toddlers. Offering smiles during a conversation lets your toddler know that you enjoy talking with them and that the conversation is meant to be fun.

Tip 6: Minimize the use of 'no.' While some limits will certainly focus on what your toddler *should* do, many will be focused on what they should *not* do. Hearing 'no' over and over again throughout the day can be exhausting for your little one. Try to talk to him in positive terms that model reasoning. For example, instead of saying 'No Michal! Don't throw your food,' you might try 'Hmmm, throwing our food makes the floor really sticky. Let's try saving it for later instead.'

Tip 7: Don't talk too much. When speaking, keep it simple. Toddlers have short attention spans, and talking too much will likely cause your toddler to lose interest. For example, one day 2-year-old Jimmy threw his toy car straight at the window in his bedroom. His mom responded by saying, 'Now Jimmy, you can't throw your toy car at the window because if you end up breaking the window we're going to have to buy a new one, and that costs a lot of money, and besides, throwing things is dangerous—what if you hurt someone? How do you think it would feel? Do you think it's nice to…' at this point, Jimmy has stopped tracking. His mother is using too many words, discussing people that aren't even present, and speaking in terms that a 2-year-old can't follow or relate to. Instead, she might say something like 'Jimmy, don't throw your toys in the house. Throwing is for outside.' At two years of age, short, direct explanations of not more than 2-3 sentences are the most likely to result in understanding.

Tip 8: Use good manners. Using 'please' and 'thank you' will model good manners for your toddler, as well as help her to see that kids and adults alike deserve respect in conversation.

Tip 9: Ask questions. Asking open-ended questions is a great way to show interest in your toddler and encourage their participation in the conversation. When trying to encourage interaction, avoid questions that can be answered with a short yes/no. Instead of asking, *'Did you go to the park with Grandma?'* ask, *'What did you do at the park?'*

Tip 10: Don't limit conversation to directions. Finally, don't just use talk to give your little one directions or feedback. Their language skills are growing a mile a minute at this age, and they are learning that language can be used for all kinds of purposes. Support this growth and create positive interaction patterns by asking them about their day, their opinions, asking them to tell stories, solve problems out loud, etc. Responses will be limited at first, but need not be any less enjoyable. You will be astounded by how quickly your toddler's language develops in just a few short years.

Effective Communication: Listening

Listening goes hand in hand with talking. It's difficult to do one effectively without the other. Being a good listener will encourage your toddler to talk and help them develop good communication skills. Remember, effective communication with your toddler is dynamic and interactive, which means modelling both talking and listening abilities.

Listening serves a number of communicative purposes, including gathering information, opening the door for empathy, building relationships, giving respect, and gaining perspective. Listening will help you to understand what is going on in your little one's mind and heart, letting you relate to them better as you help them solve problems.

Tip 1: Ask for details. When your toddler tells you about what happened at church or that her baby doll feels sad, show that you are listening by asking for more details. *What happened first? Second? Third? Why is the baby doll sad? How will you make her happy?* In addition to showing that you are listening and interested, such questions elicit new language and help your toddler to practice important cognitive functions such as recall, mental modelling, and problem solving.

Tip 2: Pay attention. In today's world, multitasking has become a way of life, even when it's unnecessary. To show your toddler that you're listening and engaged, set aside devices such as phones or tablets and give them your full attention.

Tip 3: Use active listening. Active listening refers to listening that is purposeful and fully engaged. During active listening, you are fully focused on what is being said. Body language cues, including eye contact, mirroring facial expressions, and an attentive posture all contribute to active listening. When you listen actively, your toddler will be more likely to feel that what they have to say is important, and they will be encouraged to speak more.

Tip 4: Be physically interactive. High fives, hugs, and gestures are all great ways to show that you are listening and interested in what your toddler is saying. Getting bodies involved will also make the conversation more engaging and meaningful.

Tip 5: Give unconditional love. Toddlers seriously lack in impulse control and often don't know how to express themselves in socially appropriate ways. They may speak out of anger and even say things like *'I hate you'* or *'You're ugly.'*

Remember, don't take it personally! No matter how your toddler speaks to you or what the content of their message is, make sure that they always know that you love them, no matter what. Unconditional love creates a safe space in which toddlers are able to speak freely and make mistakes without fear of losing your love or affection. This freedom will do wonders for their language skills, confidence, and trust in you as a parent.

How to deal with "I don't want..."

We've heard it a thousand times: *no.* Or, *I don't want (insert activity/behavior/food choice here).* Although '*no*' can be frustrating, it's actually a healthy part of your toddler's development. Saying '*no,*' or '*I don't want to,*' is often a toddler's way of expressing autonomy and inserting power over his own life. It's important that phrases like '*I don't want -- -*' are acknowledged, even welcomed. When toddlers see that their thoughts and opinions are important and respected, their growing individuality and independence are supported.

However, acknowledging the '*no*' doesn't mean giving in to it! As parents, we must learn to acknowledge while still setting limits and teaching appropriate behavior. For example, if little Sarah says, '*No, I don't want to turn off the tv,*' we can validate her contribution to the communication by saying calmly, '*The tv is really fun, isn't it? Sometimes I wish we could watch it all day long. You must feel a little sad that it's time to turn it off.*' This can be followed up by reinforcing the boundary: '*But too much tv takes our time away from other fun stuff, so that's why we only watch it for a little while. TV time is over, but now it's time to get ready for dinner.*'

Using this method, your toddler may still continue to say no, may even throw a tantrum, but they understand that their feelings on the matter were worth listening to. This also helps them to realize that the limit was enforced for a definable reason that always exists, and not because mom didn't understand what they wanted.

After listening, acknowledging, and then reinforcing the limit, be prepared to call on your toolkit of discipline strategies to help your toddler transition to keeping the limit. In chapter 5, we will go over a number of such strategies that will help you navigate the *'nos'* and *'I don't want tos'* with less stress and more success.

Chapter 4:

How to Solve Conflicts

As your toddler increases in independence and begins to exert her will on the world around her, she will inevitably experience conflict. Conflicts may occur with siblings, other children, and with adults—including yourself!

Helping your baby learn to manage conflict in safe and healthy ways is vital to his development. Many parents feel that toddlers aren't cognitively developed enough to learn how to solve conflicts, instead opting to solve conflicts for their toddlers whenever possible. While there will be times when the most safe or appropriate action is for you to take care of a problem from your position as caregiver, there will also be many times when conflicts are an opportunity for you to teach your toddler basic skills in self-regulation, communication, and social interaction that will provide a solid foundation for more complex situations in the future.

The best way to help toddlers learn how to handle conflict is to allow them to experience it safely, with guidance and support when needed. When done effectively, taking advantage of these teaching moments to help your toddler learn how to get along with others will contribute to her sense of self, improve her ability to self-regulate, increase her social awareness, and help her develop empathy.

The first step in helping toddlers navigate conflict is to be good examples of how to use effective communication and conflict resolution strategies ourselves. Toddlers who see parents yell, argue, become rude or mean, call names, slam doors, etc. are more likely to do those things. Modelling healthy and productive strategies for conflict resolution helps toddlers to develop healthier and more productive strategies themselves.

However, modelling goes beyond simple behavior. It's also a good idea to model thought processes in the moments surrounding conflict. For example, during a stressful encounter at the bank teller drive through window, one mother looked in the rearview mirror to see her toddler looking at her with wide eyes. Chagrined, she realized that she'd been more than a little short with the teller. Before the teller returned to the window, mom pulled out a quick think-aloud strategy: *'Boy, it makes me a little mad that this lady can't help me,'* she said. *'But I should be kind so that we can figure out the problem together. I think I'll take a deep breath. Will you help me?'* She and her toddler took a deep breath together and when the teller returned, mom finished the transaction much more calmly. By using a think-aloud strategy, she was able to model positive thought processes that take place in real-world conflict resolution.

As adults, we are often able to resolve conflicts without much help from others. But what about toddlers? How much should we help them solve conflict?

Toddlers, especially 3-year-olds, are quick to turn to mom to solve conflicts for them. Your response to these requests may range from complete intervention in the case of safety issues, to prompts and guidance as toddlers learn to handle conflict themselves, to being aware but hands-off as you let your little one try to solve the problem on his own.

As long as safety isn't an issue, a good rule of thumb is to let your toddler try to work it out on her own. Doing so will give her the experience needed to internalize successful conflict resolution strategies. However, as you move your toddler towards increased independence in handling conflict, you will still need to stay aware of the situation at hand and be ready to offer guidance in the skills, strategies, and coping mechanisms needed to stay safe, respect others, and reach her goals.

As you help your toddler learn to deal with conflict, keep the following tips and strategies in mind:

Take a break. Teach your child that sometimes, conflict can be made easier by taking a break to calm down. In the beginning, you can simply remove them from conflict situations that have escalated (for example, a tantrum in response to a problem sharing with another child). Tell them that they '*need a break to calm down*' and can come back when they're ready. Before they come back to the situation, make sure they understand why they took a break—to calm down. Later, you can move on to asking them, '*do you need a break?*' when emotions start to escalate, encouraging them to regulate their emotions with more independence. Eventually, they may even 'take a break' of their own accord.

Encourage 'I' statements. Teach older toddlers to express the problem from their own point of view, and to listen to the point of view of others. For example, *'I felt sad when you didn't want to color with me because I just wanted to color too. So I took your crayons to make you mad.'* Learning to clearly state and understand the problem will help your toddler understand where conflict has arisen from. It will also help him to become more aware of his own reactions. When the problem is clearly stated, you can encourage your toddler to think about alternative choices for dealing with the problem, whether it originated in himself or another.

Make apologies. Encouraging toddlers to apologize after a conflict has been resolved helps them learn to take responsibility for their actions. It can also help them to reset after some intense emotions. When your child is 1, they probably won't be making apologies of their own although you can model this behavior for them. When they are 2, apologies may consist simply of a single word: *'sorry.'* Once your toddler is three, you can usually start directing them towards more meaningful apologies that acknowledge what was done wrong and what will done be better next time.

Problem-solve. If your toddler comes to you asking for help with a conflict, you may want to encourage them to solve the problem themselves. Validate their feelings and ask open-ended questions to get them thinking about what they could do to resolve the conflict. For example, *'Wow, I understand that she took your toy. That sounds really frustrating. How could we get it back? How could we find a way to share?'* You might suggest compromise strategies or offer guidance, but try to let your toddler choose how to solve the problem. Afterwards, praise them for figuring it out themselves.

Step back. Allow your little one to solve her own conflicts whenever possible. Taking a step back will give him the opportunity to learn from experience. However, that doesn't mean that you aren't aware or active in keeping an eye on the situation. Be ready to offer guidance if needed, but try not to take over unless necessary.

Be safe. Not all conflicts are benign. Watch out for safety issues and intervene immediately if necessary. During the toddler years, you'll especially want to watch out for thrown objects, pushing, hitting, biting, etc. If emotions or behaviors escalate and become unsafe for anyone involved, you may need to remove your child from the interaction. Usually, you can stop things from reaching that point by being aware of the situation and intervening before it gets out of hand.

Acknowledge both sides. If your toddler and a sibling or another child come to you together for help resolving a conflict, don't take sides. Encourage each participant to share their feelings and come up with ideas for solving the problem. Even if one child is clearly in the wrong, make sure that both leave the interaction with their respect intact.

Chapter 5:

Discipline Strategies

     Much toddler discipline revolves around the use of positive and negative consequences. Positive consequences are used when you want your child to repeat a behavior, like when you want her to pick up her own toys every evening. Positive consequences include praise, rewards, and attention. They let your child know that you like what she's doing. Negative consequences, on the other hand, are used when you want your child to stop a certain behavior, like when you want to him to stop coloring on the walls. Negative consequences include ignoring, distraction, and time-outs. They let your child know that you do not like what he has done.

     Let's take a look at some effective discipline strategies.

Ignoring: Sometimes, toddlers misbehave simply to get your attention. Ignoring your child's behavior will eventually help them realize that tantrums, yelling, and demanding are not effective ways to get their needs met. In many cases, simply ignoring your toddler while they are misbehaving in this way is enough to get them to stop. When using this strategy, do not talk to or look at your toddler while the behavior is happening. Ignoring works best for tantrums, interruption, and whining. This strategy is best for ages 18 months and up.

Distraction: Distraction means to get your toddler to focus on something else. Once she is distracted, the unwanted behavior will stop by default. For example, if your toddler is crying for an extra treat after lunch, you might play a game, look out the window together and have her point at every animal she sees, or read a quick story together. This strategy works at any age of toddlerhood.

Natural consequences: Natural consequences are consequences that occur directly because of what we have done. For example, if your toddler gets angry and tears up her paper, she no longer has a paper to draw on. Sometimes, it's best to allow natural consequences to take place to help toddlers learn. However, natural consequences should not be dangerous. Always intervene if safety is at stake, and don't allow your little one to engage in behaviors that put them at risk for harm. This strategy is best for ages 2 and up.

Delay: Delaying may be used to promote good behavior or discourage unhelpful behavior. For example, you might say, '*When you've picked up your toys, we can read a story,*' or '*If we don't finish lunch soon, we'll have to wait until tomorrow to go outside.*' This strategy can work for toddlers ages 2 and up, but becomes increasingly effective as the toddler's cognitive and language abilities develop.

Removal of privileges: Removing privileges works best when what is removed is related to the behavior in questions. For example, taking away a toy that was thrown across the room. In most cases, your toddler should be able to get the privilege back after a set period of time, so long as they have either demonstrated that they are able to behave differently or that they are ready to try again. This strategy works best for toddlers 2 and up.

Time-out: Time-outs give your toddler a chance to calm down. For a time-out to be effective, you should remove from toddler wherever he is misbehaving. Many parents find that having a specific place in the house for time-outs works best. The time-out area should be free of distractions and relaxing. For toddlers, time-outs need not be long; often 2-5 minutes is enough to change the behavior and help your little one switch gears. This strategy works best for toddlers aged 2 and up.

Social rewards: Social rewards are things like praise, hugs, and high-fives as opposed to material rewards such as candy. Social rewards tend to be more powerful in the long run because they make you and your toddler partners in success. They also help to build trust and emotional currency. This strategy works for all ages of toddlerhood.

Sticker charts: Formal reward systems, such as a sticker chart, can make things like picking up toys and eating lunch feel like a game. Sticker charts also help toddlers feel powerful as they watch their own progress. This strategy is most effective for toddlers aged 3 and up.

Toddlers have pretty short attention spans, so it's important to give consequences, whether positive or negative, right after a behavior has occurred. This way, they can remember what it is that you do or do not like and more easily make connections between the cause and effect of behavior and consequence.

Keep in mind that negative consequences should never be used punitively or handed out in anger. Negative consequences help to reduce unsafe or unhelpful behaviors, but are never intended to hurt or punish your toddler.

When using consequences to discourage unsafe or unhelpful behavior, the CDC recommends the following five steps:

> *Step 1:* Identify the misbehavior.
> *Step 2:* Give a warning.
> *Step 3:* Give a consequence.
> *Step 4:* Tell them why.
> *Step 5:* Go back to positive communication.

Step 1: Identify the misbehavior. By alerting your toddler to the misbehavior, you are reminding them of expectations and giving them the chance to choose to change the behavior on their own.

Step 2: Give a warning. A warning further reminds your toddler that the misbehavior will have consequences and provides motivation should they need help making the decision to stop. A warning also encourages them to think about cause and effect in an actionable way.

Step 3: Give a consequence. The consequence should be proportionate to the misbehavior and the toddler's development, and should be aimed at helping the toddler to recognize that the behavior is not effective or desirable.

Step 4: Tell them why. Make sure that your toddler understands why the consequence happened, either at the time or immediately after. Help them to make connections between the behavior and the consequence.

Step 5: Go back to positive communication. Once the consequence is over, provide positive interaction in the form of talk, hugs, or help to 'try again.' This will reassure your toddler that you love them and you are helping them to learn so that they and/or others can stay safe and healthy. Always go back to being positive.

As you follow the strategies in this chapter, you'll find that your individual toddler responds better to some methods than to others. While these strategies are usually considered gentle and effective, if anything seems to cause your little one stress and anxiety beyond what is normal for their age, stop and try a different one.

Chapter 6: 10 Common Mistakes

and How to Avoid Them

Every parent makes mistakes when it comes to child-rearing, and you will no doubt experience your share. However, mistakes need not be considered a disaster. Far from it, conscientious parenting will help to turn many mistakes into important learning experiences. Even so, it can be frustrating to realize that a thoughtful strategy has actually been making a discipline problem *worse*. Knowledge is power, so let's take a look at some of the most common toddler discipline mistakes and how to avoid them.

Giving in to whining. It's often tempting to capitulate when your toddler won't stop whining for that favorite treat or more time at the park. However, giving in only teaches your little one that whining is an effective tool for reaching goals. It also lets them know that the limit which brought on the whining isn't actually that important—that mom is willing to forget it given enough requests.

Instead of giving in to whining, firmly but gently remind your toddler what the limit is and why it's in place. Use simple language and don't overexplain. If your toddler continues to whine, try distracting them with a different activity, ask for their help, or give them an interesting task to complete. If the whining still doesn't stop, acknowledge your child's feelings and enact a productive consequence. For example, you might say *'I'm sorry, but we're not going to stay outside right now because outside time is over. I can see that it's really disappointing, but whining isn't the right way to handle it. I'd like you to spend five minutes in your quiet place so that you can calm down.'*

Lying. Sometimes it's all too easy to tell a white lie to keep kids in line. My neighbor once told her little boy that the ice-cream truck played music when it was *out* of ice-cream! However, kids will eventually catch on—and when they do, you will lose emotional currency. Toddlers need to be able to trust that their parents are being honest about how the world works. Lying is a quick fix that will eventually catch up with us, and nixes many opportunities for children to learn the healthy skills needed to deal with reality.

Inconsistency. Another pitfall of guiding your little one through toddlerhood is inconsistency. The parental zeal you felt when you established a new routine or set a new limit on Tuesday may have given way to exhaustion by Friday—at which point it's all too easy to let the new structure slide. Inconsistency can undermine your toddler's view of your reliability as well as the positive behaviors you are trying to teach her. Her behaviors may become worse as she learns that she can 'get away with it,' and she may experience stress from not knowing what to expect. Even though it can be challenging, try to remain as consistent as possible with toddler discipline. It will pay off in the long run for both of you.

Bribes. Bribery is often an effective short-term solution, and on occasion it may be your best course of action. However, bribery rarely teaches or reinforces underlying principles of behavior and citizenship that your toddle needs to develop. Bribery can cut short teaching opportunities that may have provided your toddler with valuable insight and helped them practice making positive choices. Whenever possible, try to motivate your little one with positive reinforcement (hugs, smiles, high-fives) and discipline rather than bribes. Doing so will help them to internalize the behaviors you are trying to teach and develop an understanding of why those behaviors are expected.

Talking too much. As amazing as your toddler's developing language abilities are, they aren't quite ready for drawn out or overly complicated explanations. Make sure to speak in simple, clear terms appropriate to your toddler's age. Over-explaining or talking too much can lead to boredom, tuning-out, or confusion, all of which may make discipline problems worse.

Poor follow-through. Sometimes, adults tell toddlers that they'll play with them 'later' or get them from their play room in 10 minutes when in fact, the adult is simply trying to appease the toddler so that they can get back to what their doing. However, this undermines your toddlers trust in your reliability. It's important to avoid making promises that you aren't able to keep. For example, if your toddler is insisting on a story during a particularly busy afternoon, it can be tempting to tell them *'sure, we can read the book in a little while,'* just to get them to stop asking. However, if you're not actually able to read the book later, it's better just to be honest. Try saying, *'I know how much you love that book. I would love to read it together, but today is really busy. Let's read it tonight or tomorrow. Which one would you like?'*

Reacting. Reacting is far less effective than responding in most situations. If you find it difficult to step away from a reaction in a stressful situation, try building up your personal toolbox of strategies for dealing stress. Motherhood can be challenging, frustrating, and at times incredibly overwhelming. It's important to have healthy coping strategies to reduce frustration and help us to get back on track in difficult moments. Breathing, counting to 10, and calmly expressing our own feelings in non-aggressive ways can all be helpful in moving away from reacting. This will be discussed further in the next chapter.

Not enough expressions of love. We all express love in different ways. Some people grow up in families where hugs and I love yous were exchanged freely, while others used subtler ways to communicate their feelings. At one point in time, it was considered developmentally healthy to refrain from giving your toddler too many overt expressions of love, lest they fail to 'toughen up' against the realities of life. However, many years of research in child development has shown that toddlers need love to thrive. Make sure that your toddler knows that you love him, including through hugs, smiles, and words.

Chapter 7:

Secrets of Staying Calm

It's no secret that parenting is hard. Between loss of sleep, constantly paying attention, tantrums, refusals, and what can feel like a thousand other spinning plates, it's inevitable that you will experience frustration as a parent.

However, for your own health and the health of your baby, it is helpful to learn how to remain calm in the face of toddler discipline problems. In this chapter, we will go over some important strategies to help you stay during your child's most frustrating moments. With this information in hand, you will be able to navigate the ups and downs of toddlerhood with more efficiency and fewer grey hairs!

Don't react, respond. When Marissa's 3-year-old son Alex got angry and knocked his bowl of spaghetti off the table, her first instinct was to start yelling. It had been a long week and she was near her wits end. As the spaghetti hit the floor, all she wanted to do was snap at her son, toss him in his room, and close the door without another word. Alternatively, she could take a deep breath, remind him gently but firmly that throwing food on the floor was not okay, and put him in time out to calm down before helping him clean up the mess.

In the first case, Marissa would have been simply *reacting* to her son's behavior. Reactions are often only moderately predictable at best, and may be more about protecting our own emotional state than helping our toddlers learn. To simply react is to indulge our first impulse in the face of frustration. It's almost always better to *respond* to misbehavior than to react. In the second scenario, Marissa would first recognize that she was about to react, then give herself a give herself a second to breathe and make choices about how to handle the situation. Reacting takes away our parenting choices, while responding is all about those choices.

Remember that you're the one in control. When a toddler acts out in defiance or refuses to do as they're asked, it's not uncommon for a stressed parent to feel like the toddler is the one in control of the situation. Feeling out of control can be just as negative for parents as it is for little ones. Remembering that you are the one in control can help you to take a breath and re-evaluate before taking action.

Never take it personally. Yes, it is possible for parents to get their feelings hurt! When your two-year-old twists away from your hug with an angry '*No!*' or gleefully dumps out the box you just asked her not to touch, it can sometimes be tempting to take such behavior as a personal affront. As your child learns to self-regulate, they will sometimes get mad at you, lash out in frustration, and may even say unkind things towards you.

Taking these behaviors personally will only make it harder for you to identify and deliver the most effective responses and discipline strategies. If you find your emotions getting caught up in the drama, take a moment to step back and breathe or ask a partner to take over while you calm down. Maintaining perspective will help you to navigate your toddler's behavior with less stress and more success.

Count to ten. If you find yourself about to react rather than respond, have a sudden flash of emotion at the end of a long day, or simply need to control a giggle when your toddler misbehaves oh-so-cutely, take a moment to count to ten and let the impulses pass.

Don't try to 'fix' everything. Remember, you want to foster your toddler's ability to solve her own problems in healthy and constructive ways. This means sometimes taking a step back and offering encouragement instead of direct intervention. These strategies aren't just important for your toddler, they're also important for your own sanity. The parent who is constantly on guard, swooping in to fix every difficulty or conflict that arises, is more likely to experience stress, exhaustion, and burn out. She is also more likely to feel anxious that a toddler's 'mistakes' are her fault, instead of viewing them as exciting steps in the process of growth.

Be consistent. Consistency is an important parenting strategy, but it also benefits mom. When you are consistent in your efforts to provide discipline, your toddler will likely experience less frustration and act out less over time, which means frustration for you as well. You can also feel good knowing that you are helping your toddler learn to be safe and productive.

Keep the big picture in mind. It can be easy to feel overwhelmed in some of the more difficult moments of toddler discipline. It can help to take comfort in remembering two things: First, *what you are doing matters*. Second, *toddlerhood doesn't last forever.*

Plan for breaks and 'me' time. Regardless of whether you're a full-time caregiver or juggling parenting and a career, it's important to plan time for yourself. By giving yourself breaks and time to relax, unwind, and get some needed mental space, you will return to your toddler with more to give. You will be able to experience the joys of parenting more fully and handle the frustrations more effectively.

Get enough sleep. Lack of sleep is a common issue faced by parents, even when babies become toddlers. If you find yourself struggling to get enough shut-eye, you might try setting up a play-group exchange that would allow you to get a couple of extra hours' nap time once or twice a week, or plan to take naps while your little one is sleeping. Although it can be tempting to stay up late to get things done, you may benefit from an earlier bedtime when possible. Having enough shuteye will make you more mentally alert and emotionally resilient.

Chapter 8:

Tying It All Together

We've gone over some exciting information in this book! Toddlerhood can be a challenging but truly rewarding time with your little one. We hope that you will take what you've learned and use it to create an effective, healthy environment for your toddler to grow in.

Keep in mind that none of the topics covered in this book are meant to be treated in isolation. Each facet of toddler discipline works with the others—brain development influencing strategies, strategies creating a positive environment, a positive environment helping toddler and mom to stay calm, calmness creating a space for more effective strategies. Each aspect supports the others in an improved and increasingly effective whole.

As you move through the toddler years, you will need to experiment, adapt and try new things as your child's needs change. It's an exciting time of life, one that will definitely keep you on your toes as your toddler makes strides in cognitive development, language abilities, social interaction, and emotional intelligence.

So that's it Supermoms! We hope that you will find the insights, strategies and tips in this book helpful as you work to effectively teach your children positive behaviors, emotional regulation, and social skills. We also hope that this introduction to toddler discipline will make a positive difference in how you experience these amazing formative years. Although this time in your child's life can be challenging, it can also be immensely rewarding. By reading this guide you have taken the first step towards a successful and enjoyable toddlerhood.

You may also like…

Baby sleep is not a science anymore!

This Baby Sleep book is a part of the Supermom Series created for the busy new moms, who want to give their child the very best. It describes the most effective and **gentle no-cry sleep solutions for your child's sleep problems.**

Find it on Amazon.com
https://www.amazon.com/dp/B01N4BVU16

Essential Baby Food Guide for Supermoms!

We'll be covering the basics of how to safely introduce your little one to first foods, and how to avoid common roadblocks to baby food success.

We've even put together 25 Baby Food Recipes for easy reference when you want to pull together a nutritious and delicious meal for your growing baby. You will find homemade organic recipes of baby purees, porridges and soups with easy-to-follow instructions.

Find it on Amazon.com
hhttps://www.amazon.com/dp/B01MSE281Z

Thank You for Buying My Book!

Your Free Gift

Funny Riddles for Children

https://supermomseries.wixsite.com/riddles

Download it now!